SPOT 50
Butterflies
& Moths

Camilla de la Bedoyere

Miles
KeLLY

First published in 2011 by Miles Kelly Publishing Ltd
Harding's Barn, Bardfield End Green, Thaxted, Essex, CM6 3PX, UK

This edition printed in 2015

2 4 6 8 10 9 7 5 3

Publishing Director Belinda Gallagher

Creative Director Jo Cowan

Editors Amanda Askew, Sarah Parkin

Editorial Assistant Lauren White

Designer Kayleigh Allen

Production Elizabeth Collins, Caroline Kelly

Reprographics Stephan Davis, Jennifer Cozens, Lorraine King

Assets Lorraine King

ISBN 978-1-84810-597-3

Printed in China

British Library Cataloguing-in-Publication Data
A catalogue record for this book is available from the British Library

ACKNOWLEDGEMENTS
The publishers would like to thank the artists Mike Atkinson,
Andrea Morandi and Mike Saunders who have contributed to this book

The publishers would like to thank the following sources for the use of their photographs:
Fotolia.com 4(bl) MLA Photography
Shutterstock.com 4(tl) Martina I. Meyer, (tr) David Benton, (br) AdamEdwards

All other images are from the Miles Kelly Archives

Made with paper from a sustainable forest

www.mileskelly.net
info@mileskelly.net

CONTENTS

Tick the circles when you have spotted the species.

A BUTTERFLY & MOTH GARDEN

Butterflies and moths pollinate plants, which means they play **an important part in helping gardens to grow.** These insects feed on the sugary nectar that is made by flowers. A butterfly and moth garden needs lots of different types of flowers, so there is a range from spring through to late autumn.

This is a small tortoiseshell butterfly. Scented plants such as oregano are popular food plants.

This is a comma butterfly. Michaelmas daisies provide nectar in the autumn.

• Butterflies especially like the nectar of flowers from oregano, lavender, Michaelmas daisies and buddleia, which attract them to gardens.

• Plants with a strong evening scent, such as nicotiana, evening primrose, honeysuckle and jasmine, will attract moths to the garden.

• Put flat stones or rocks in sunny spots of the garden. Butterflies will come and rest on them to bask in the summer sun.

• Avoid tidying the garden too much for winter. Some butterflies and moths bury themselves under shrubs, in ivy or in sheds, to sleep through the winter.

Buddleia is so popular with butterflies like these peacocks that it is often called the butterfly bush.

Lavender attracts pollinating insects, such as this small white butterfly, especially when grown in full sun.

ANATOMY

Butterflies and moths have wings that are covered in scales, two large compound eyes and special mouthparts. Most moths are nocturnal, which means they are active at night. Butterflies are usually more colourful than moths and are most active in the day.

The mouthpart is called a proboscis, and is used to take nectar from flowers

Two antennae are used to sense smell and touch

Large compound eyes have many lenses

One pair of forewings

Wingspan is measured across the widest part of the forewings

Insect bodies are divided into three parts — head, thorax and abdomen

One pair of hind wings

BUTTERFLY

Wings are usually held upright when resting

Colourful, patterned wings

Antennae have rounded clubs on the tips

Body is usually smooth and slender

MOTH

Antennae are usually thin, or broad and feathery

Body is usually plump and furry

Wings are usually held flat over the body when resting

Wings are often dull in colour

ADONIS BLUE

Male adonis blue butterflies are stunning, with bright-blue wings. Females are chocolate-brown in colour and harder to recognize. The eggs are laid on horseshoe vetch – a grassland plant that becomes the food of the larvae when they hatch, two weeks later. The larvae are green with yellow stripes and can survive the winter. Adults feed on marjoram and ragwort.

ACTUAL SIZE

Adonis blue butterflies live in the south and east of England. They need warmth and shelter to survive.

FACT FILE

Scientific name
Lysandra bellargus

Habitat Warm, sheltered grasslands

Breeding There are two broods – in spring and late summer

Wingspan 3 to 4 cm

Males have brilliant blue wings (females are chocolate-brown)

Broad, hairy body

Dark-blue band

White fringe

Small, black spots or streaks

BRIMSTONE

These butterflies are widespread around Britain and other parts of Europe and North Africa. The bluish-green caterpillars feed on buckthorn leaves and the adults live on a diet of nectar from flowers such as buddleia. The adults emerge from their chrysalises in July and live until the following summer, after a winter hibernation.

ACTUAL SIZE

Females lay their eggs on the underside of buckthorn leaves, so the caterpillars emerge to a ready supply of food.

FACT FILE

Scientific name
Gonepteryx rhamni

Habitat Woodland and scrub

Breeding Eggs are laid in May, larvae pupate in June/July and adults emerge two weeks later

Wingspan Up to 6 cm

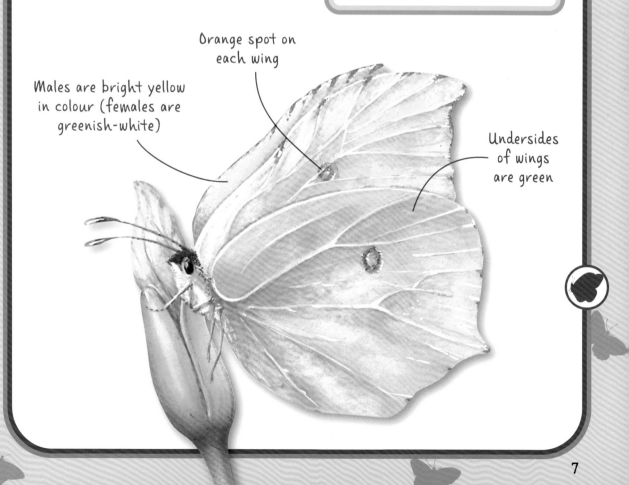

Orange spot on each wing

Males are bright yellow in colour (females are greenish-white)

Undersides of wings are green

BROWN ARGUS

Some butterflies can travel considerable distances, but these butterflies rarely wander more than a few hundred metres. They prefer regions in southern Britain with chalky grasslands and favour warm, sheltered places. Adults may be seen fluttering around their food plants – marjoram, thyme, white clover and ragwort.

ACTUAL SIZE

The green larvae are striped and hairy. They feed on the underside of leaves, creating thin patches that can be seen from above.

FACT FILE

Scientific name *Aricia agestis*

Habitat Downs, heaths and woodlands

Breeding Eggs are laid one at a time, and hatch after about one week

Wingspan 2.5 to 3 cm

Blue sheen in certain lights

White fringe

Orange spots

Blue-brown, hairy body

CLOUDED YELLOW

These orange-yellow butterflies were originally from Africa and Europe, but are now regularly sighted in the British Isles. While most clouded yellows still fly in from abroad, they are able to survive the winter here, especially if the weather remains mild. When they settle, they hold their wings upright. Found throughout the UK and Ireland, they are most common in England and Wales.

ACTUAL SIZE

Clouded yellow larvae are green and well-camouflaged. They moult four times before pupating.

FACT FILE

Scientific name *Colias croceus*

Habitat Coasts, farms, parks, fields, heaths and grasslands

Breeding Many yellow eggs are laid in a brood and turn orange, hatching after one week

Wingspan 5.5 to 6.5 cm

Black border around wings

Bright-yellow wings with lemon-yellow undersides

Orange-and-black spots on each wing

COMMA

With dull patterns on the underside of their wings, commas can be difficult to see among dead leaves. This camouflage helps protect the butterflies from predators when they overwinter and hang from leaves. Commas live in gardens and woodlands where they can find flowers to supply them with leaves as larvae and nectar as adults.

ACTUAL SIZE

The larvae are black with red-and-white markings, giving them the appearance of bird droppings. They are covered in spines.

FACT FILE

Scientific name
Polygonia c-album

Habitat Gardens and meadows

Breeding Two broods each year

Wingspan 4 to 5.5 cm

Long, slender antennae

Long, sucking mouthparts (proboscis)

Furry body

Orange-brown wings with dark markings

Ragged edges to wings

COMMON BLUE

These pretty butterflies are most likely to be seen between May and September, when they feed on nectar. They are most common around large, flat-headed flowers, especially near roadsides or meadows. The larvae are green with yellow stripes along their sides and a dark line down their backs. They feed on the leaves of plants, such as white clover and bird's-foot trefoil.

ACTUAL SIZE

The larvae produce a substance from their skin that attracts ants, and in turn, the ants protect the larvae from predators.

FACT FILE

Scientific name
Polyommatus icarus

Habitat Grasslands, dunes and wastelands

Breeding Larvae are small and green

Wingspan 3 to 4 cm

Males have violet-blue upperwings and females have brown

Thin, black border

Undersides of wings are grey or beige

Long antennae

Orange markings and black spots on the undersides

Blue colouring near the body

DARK GREEN FRITILLARY

These butterflies are mostly orange and black, but they get their name from the dark-green tinge on the undersides of their wings. They are found throughout Britain, except most of Scotland and the Isle of Man. Adults emerge from their pupae in June, and they are strong fliers that dart from flower to flower, sucking nectar. After the larvae hatch, they rest until spring when they start feeding.

ACTUAL SIZE

There are many types of fritillary butterflies. Most of them have orange-brown wings with black checks.

FACT FILE

Scientific name *Argynnis aglaja*

Habitat Open grassland, woodlands and coastal areas

Breeding Each female can lay hundreds of yellow eggs in a single brood.

Wingspan Up to 7 cm

Large, hairy body

Black spots cover the wings

Males have larger bodies than females

Undersides have a hint of green

GRAYLING

These quite large butterflies can be easily spotted when in flight. However, once graylings settle on sand, mud or rocks they become almost invisible. These insects prefer sunny, dry spots and the adults are active from June to the middle of September. They are most common along coasts, especially in England and Wales. Caterpillars feed on grasses and are brown and cream in colour.

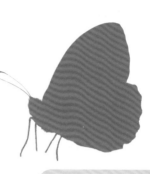

ACTUAL SIZE

Graylings are becoming rare in Britain. The populations are becoming smaller, and they are found in fewer habitats than ever before.

FACT FILE

Scientific name
Hipparchia semele

Habitat Dunes, coastal paths, cliffs and hedges

Breeding White eggs are laid one at a time

Wingspan Up to 6 cm

Long antennae

When settled, wings are closed and orange parts may be hidden

Dark eye-spots on forewings

Mottled brown underside

GREEN HAIRSTREAK

Males and females look similar, but can be told apart by their behaviour. Males usually stay in their territories, waiting for females to pass by. Females are very active, fluttering between flowers looking for food, or searching for places to lay their eggs. The larvae are short and stubby. They feed on leaves and buds, but as they age they may feed on each other.

ACTUAL SIZE

When the pupae are disturbed they can make a noise loud enough to be heard by the human ear.

FACT FILE

Scientific name *Callophrys rubi*

Habitat Hedgerows, moors, hillsides, wasteland and heaths

Breeding Eggs are laid one at a time and hatch after one or two weeks

Wingspan 2.5 to 3.5 cm

The tops of the wings are brown, but they are only seen in flight

Faint line of white spots

Green underwings provide good camouflage

GREEN-VEINED WHITE

These butterflies are widespread, but they are not often seen in gardens. Green-veined whites mostly feed on wild plants found in hedgerows, along riverbanks and open grasslands. The sexes look similar except for their black spots. Females usually have two spots on each forewing, while males have just one, which may be very faint. Green larvae hatch from little white eggs, and feed on leaves.

ACTUAL SIZE

Males often gather around mud, where they can find nutrients to eat. This is known as 'mud-puddling'.

FACT FILE

Scientific name *Pieris napi*

Habitat Damp places, grasslands and sheltered places

Breeding Eggs are laid singly and hatch in about a week

Wingspan 4 to 5 cm

Wings are white with some spots

Long antennae

Hind wings have bold green streaks

HOLLY BLUE

Holly blue butterflies are found flying around holly bushes in spring, where females lay their eggs. The larvae, which are small and green, feed on holly flower buds. When they mature, this first brood mates to produce a second brood and the eggs are usually laid on ivy. The second group of adults is able to survive winter as chrysalises, or pupae.

ACTUAL SIZE

Adults feed on sap from plants and the sticky substance made by aphids.

FACT FILE

Scientific name
Celastrina argiolus

Habitat Woodlands, parks and gardens

Breeding Two broods every summer

Wingspan 3 to 4 cm

Broad, black borders to wings in females (narrower in males)

Pale, violet-blue wings

Antennae have small, white stripes

Underside of wings is pale grey-blue with black spots

LARGE HEATH

It is difficult to spot large heath butterflies as they prefer damp habitats where it is hard to walk. In northern Scotland they tend to have fewer spots on their wings than those that live elsewhere. Larvae feed on a range of wild plants, including watercress, hedge mustard and cuckooflower. Adults suck nectar from flowers such as bugle and buttercups. Pupation takes about ten days, although some pupae survive through winter.

ACTUAL SIZE

The large heath butterflies in northern areas tend to have fewer spots on their wings than those in southern places.

FACT FILE

Scientific name
Coenonympha tullia
Habitat Lowlands such as heaths, bogs and moorlands
Breeding Eggs are laid singly and take around two weeks to hatch
Wingspan Up to 4 cm

Black eye-spots on both forewings and hind wings

Resting butterflies have their wings closed

Hairy body

LARGE SKIPPER

During June and July, large skippers fly around flowering plants in search of nectar to feed on, and lay only one brood of eggs. They particularly like bramble and thistles. Males are territorial, and will chase away other males that stray into their area. It is difficult to find the green larvae, which hide within 'tents' made of folded blades of grass. Large skippers are widespread in England and Wales.

ACTUAL SIZE

Males have dark bands on their forewings, which are made up from special scent glands. They help males to attract females.

FACT FILE

Scientific name *Ochlodes faunus*

Habitat Sheltered grasslands, parks and hedgerows

Breeding Females normally lay their white eggs during the early afternoon

Wingspan 3 to 3.5 cm

Males have a thick, dark band in the centre of the forewing

Large eyes

Deep orange-brown colour

Patches of pale-orange or gold on forewings

LARGE WHITE

These butterflies are often seen fluttering around cabbage and brussel sprout plants. These garden crops are favourite foods of the yellow-and-black larvae, and the undersides are often coated with patches of yellow eggs. When the larvae hatch, they can munch through entire leaves. Larvae that hatch late in the season form pupae to survive the winter, emerging as adults in April.

ACTUAL SIZE

Many large whites live in Britain and Ireland throughout the year, but others fly over from Europe, and are called migrants.

FACT FILE

Scientific name *Pieris brassicae*

Habitat Gardens, farms, fields and parks

Breeding There are two or three broods a year and females lay hundreds of eggs at a time

Wingspan 6 cm

Females have two spots on forewings, males have none

Black mark on the top corner of forewing

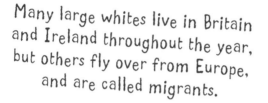

Undersides of wings are creamy-white

MARSH FRITILLARY

Small populations of these butterflies can be found around the British Isles. The larvae need warm conditions to grow. Male adults emerge from the pupae before females and set up their territories, where they wait for mates. The hairy larvae use silk to fasten the edges of leaves together. They feed inside their 'nests', relying on wild flowering plants for food.

These butterflies are one of Britain's rarest species. Their numbers have been declining for some time.

FACT FILE

Scientific name
Euphydryas aurinia
Habitat Moors, heaths and damp meadows
Breeding Hundreds of small yellow eggs are laid in June or July
Wingspan 3 to 5 cm

The surface of the wings may be shiny

Checked pattern on black background

Cream or yellow spots on upperside of wings

MEADOW BROWN

Among the most common of all British butterflies are meadow browns. Adults feed on nectar from many flowering plants, and larvae eat grasses and other fine-leaved plants. While males often flutter above vegetation, looking for mates, females rest near the ground. They usually lay their eggs one at a time and the larvae hatch two to four weeks later.

ACTUAL SIZE

When females are disturbed, they raise their forewings and flash their eye-spots to scare away any predators nearby.

FACT FILE

Scientific name *Maniola jurtina*

Habitat Most habitats, especially grasslands

Breeding Brown larvae hatch from dark eggs, and turn green as they mature

Wingspan 4 to 6 cm

Eye-spots

Forewings are mostly brown with some orange

Hind wings are brown with a pale fringe

Males are slightly darker than females

ORANGE TIP

These colourful butterflies flit around flowers in early summer, from April to June, laying their eggs. The pale eggs are long and thin, but turn orange after a few days. The green larvae feed on flowerbuds, but they will eat each other if they can. The orange tips on the males' forewings warn birds that they taste bad.

ACTUAL SIZE

Only one egg is laid at a time, so it can take a female some time to lay her whole clutch on the undersides of flowerbuds.

FACT FILE

Scientific name
Anthocharis cardamines
Habitat Gardens, meadows and hedgerows
Breeding Lays single eggs
Wingspan 4 to 5.5 cm

One black spot on forewings of both males and females

Males have large orange patch and black tips on forewings

Underside of wings is mottled green and cream for camouflage

PAINTED LADY

These big butterflies have spectacular, boldly patterned wings. They arrive from mainland Europe in spring or summer, and visit food plants in gardens and along the coasts, sucking up nectar. Their larvae can strip whole plants. Painted ladies need plenty of energy to breed, but cannot survive the British winter at any stage of their life-cycle.

ACTUAL SIZE

Painted ladies are the only butterflies known to visit Iceland. It is thought they leave Africa in search of food.

FACT FILE

Scientific name *Cynthia cardui*

Habitat Gardens, parks, coasts, farms and wasteland

Breeding Black, hairy larvae feed on underside of leaves

Wingspan 6 to 7.5 cm

Long antennae are tipped with white

Deep orangey-brown colour

Males and females look similar, with black tips and white spots on forewings

Large body

PEACOCK

Often seen on buddleia in summer, peacock butterflies wake from hibernation in spring and mate soon after. Females lay small, green eggs in batches of up to 500, often on nettles or hops – the larvae's favourite food. Adults emerge from the pupae in July and feed on nectar from flowers or on juices from over-ripe fruit. Peacock butterflies live for one year.

ACTUAL SIZE

Peacock butterflies get their name from the large patterns on their wings, which are similar to the eye-shaped patterns on the tails of peacock birds.

FACT FILE

Scientific name *Inachis io*
Habitat Flowery gardens and meadows
Breeding Fully grown larvae are about 4 cm long and they have black-and-white spots and long, black dorsal spines
Wingspan 5 to 7.5 cm

Hair on thorax

Long antennae used for smelling and touching

Four false eyes on wings

Dark-brown wing edges

PURPLE EMPEROR

Male purple emperors are among the most spectacular of British butterflies, but are rarely seen. They live in woodlands in southern England, especially those with oak and willow trees. The blue-green eggs are laid on willow trees and bushes, and their bases turn purple as they age. The larvae are well camouflaged among leaves and they feed on the spring buds.

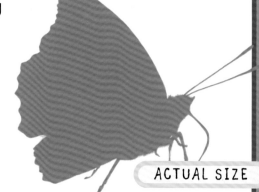

ACTUAL SIZE

Adults feed on nectar from flowers, but they also take nutrients from dead animals and animal dung.

FACT FILE

Scientific name *Apatura iris*
Habitat Woodlands
Breeding Eggs are laid high up in trees, and hatch in about ten days
Wingspan 7 to 9 cm

Black edges

Line of white spots

Males have purple sheen on their wings (females are brown)

Yellow proboscis

Eye-spots

PURPLE HAIRSTREAK

Purple hairstreaks live in oak woodlands, and their larvae feed on oak buds. They are found mostly in England, Wales and some parts of Scotland, thriving in warm conditions. They flutter in groups around treetops, searching for food, mates or places to lay their eggs. Males have a purple sheen to their wings and females have purple marks on their forewings. The pupae survive the winter in leaf litter and are often buried by ants in the soil.

ACTUAL SIZE

Eggs are laid near buds, especially on the south side of a tree where the eggs will be warmed by the sunshine.

FACT FILE

Scientific name
Neozephyrus quercus

Habitat Oak woodlands

Breeding The eggs are laid in late summer, and larvae hatch the following spring

Wingspan 3 to 4 cm

Males have dark and white borders on the forewings

Both males and females have a purple sheen

Creamy-white line on underside

Orange markings on underside

Underside is grey-brown

RED ADMIRAL

Named after their 'admirable' colours, these butterflies are easily recognized by their dark-coloured wings with red bands and white spots. Red admirals are fast, powerful fliers and – unusually for butterflies – may fly at night. These insects are found throughout the UK and Europe in a wide range of habitats.

ACTUAL SIZE

The larvae are normally dark and bristled. They may be green, grey or black, and have yellow lines on either side.

FACT FILE

Scientific name
Vanessa atalanta

Habitat Gardens and meadows

Breeding Single eggs are laid on nettle leaves

Wingspan 6 cm

Long antennae

Red bands on forewings

Edges of wings lined with blue spots

Red patches along the back of hind wings

RINGLET

Males and females are almost identical, but a slightly darker band can sometimes be seen on the males' forewings. They are quite common and live around Britain in damp or sheltered places. Unlike many other butterflies, ringlets are active in cool or cloudy weather, flying between bramble bushes or thistles to feed. Larvae are cream in colour and hairy. They feed on grasses throughout winter.

ACTUAL SIZE

Ringlets are named after small circles on their undersides. The number and size of these circles can vary.

FACT FILE

Scientific name
Aphantopus hyperantus

Habitat Woodlands, hedgerows and damp meadows

Breeding One brood a year, with adults emerging in June

Wingspan 4.5 to 5 cm

Velvety, brown wings

Eye-spots

White fringe on the wings

SMALL COPPER

These bright, colourful insects are seen throughout Britain, in many habitats. Males are often seen resting in the sunshine, on the ground or on a warm stone. They wait for passing females and fly upwards to attack any other insects that pass overhead. Eggs are usually laid on sorrel leaves, which the larvae will feast on. The short, plump larvae moult four or five times before pupating.

ACTUAL SIZE

The colours of small coppers vary and some have deep-red colours. Others even have creamy-white forewings and dark hind wings.

FACT FILE

Scientific name
Lycaena phlaeas

Habitat Grassland, moors, coastal areas, fields and gardens

Breeding There may be up to four generations in a single year

Wingspan 2.5 to 3.5 cm

Brown band near edge of wing

Orange-copper colour with brown spots

All four wings have a pale fringe

Pointed tails

SMALL HEATH

Despite their name, these butterflies are not just found in heaths. They are widespread in the British Isles and Ireland, and feed on nectar from a variety of different plants. The small, green larvae are well-hidden from view among grass stems. They usually rest during the day, and feed at night on grass tips. The larvae that hatch near the end of the summer may survive the winter and pupate in April.

ACTUAL SIZE

Females sometimes fly in a zigzag pattern over vegetation. They are looking for mates.

FACT FILE

Scientific name
Coenonympha pamphilus
Habitat Grasslands, wastelands, sand dunes and heaths
Breeding Small green-white eggs are laid one at a time on grass stems
Wingspan 3.5 cm

Eye-spot on underside of forewing

Orange patch

Usually rests with wings closed

Hind wing underside is brown, cream and grey

Furry body

SMALL SKIPPER

These small butterflies dart around between flowering plants to feed, but they lay their eggs on grass. They live throughout England and Wales, and are most active from the middle of June to August, especially on warm days. Males and females look similar, but males sometimes have small bands of dark scales on their forewings. They are also more active when searching for mates.

ACTUAL SIZE

Some insects are attracted to certain colours of flowers. Small skippers favour purple, pink and red flowers, such as thistles.

FACT FILE

Scientific name
Thymelicus sylvestris

Habitat Anywhere that grass can grow tall

Breeding Rows of up to eight eggs are laid along grass stems

Wingspan 2.5 to 3.5 cm

Antennae tips are orange-brown

Furry body

Males may have a slender, dark band on forewings

Dark-coloured hind wing

SMALL TORTOISESHELL

Named after their colouring, small tortoiseshells are often one of the first butterflies to be seen in spring. Adults emerge from hibernation in March or April and mate soon afterwards. They lay their eggs on food plants, such as nettles. The eggs then hatch about ten days later. Small tortoiseshells are common butterflies and live in a range of habitats, particularly near human homes.

ACTUAL SIZE

This butterfly's Latin name, Aglais urticae, comes from the word for nettles, urtica, the butterfly's favourite food.

FACT FILE

Scientific name *Aglais urticae*

Habitat Flowery gardens and meadows

Breeding Heaps of eggs are laid on the underside of nettle leaves in April

Wingspan 4 to 4.5 cm

Orange-and-black markings on wings

Blue markings along wing edges

Points on the edges of forewings and hind wings

SMALL WHITE

Like its cousin, the large white, this butterfly is commonly known as a **cabbage white.** Females have two black spots on each of their forewings, and males have just one. Adults suck nectar from flowers such as dandelions, and larvae eat the leaves of plants such as cabbage. Adults can often be seen flying upwards in spirals, performing mating rituals.

ACTUAL SIZE

Adults emerge from their pupae in July. They breed twice in summer and the last generation spends winter, protected from the cold, as pupae or chrysalises.

FACT FILE

Scientific name *Pieris rapae*
Habitat Gardens and fields
Breeding The larvae are green with black stripes on their backs and sides
Wingspan 4.5 cm

White, cream or pale-yellow in colour

Two black spots on each forewing

Soft body covered with bristles

Long, tube-like mouthparts

SPECKLED WOOD

These butterflies fly around woodlands and gardens in the summer months. They do not surround flowers – like many other butterflies do – because they do not feed on nectar. Instead they feed on the sugary substance made by aphids. Females lay single eggs on grasses, which the larvae feed on when they hatch. The larvae eat and moult for about ten days before turning into chrysalises.

ACTUAL SIZE

Males fiercely defend their territories from rival males. They can sometimes be seen fighting, with their wings clashing.

FACT FILE

Scientific name
Pararge aegeria

Habitat Woodlands and gardens

Breeding Larvae are green

Wingspan 4 cm

Forewings have one black eye-spot

Slender antennae

Wings are mottled brown with creamy markings

Brown, furry body

Hind wings have a row of three black eye-spots

SWALLOWTAIL

Britain's largest butterflies are **attractive insects.** Their name describes the long 'tails' that grow at the back of their hind wings. The larvae resembles bird droppings, which puts off predators. As they grow, the larvae turn green and black with orange marks, and produce a foul smell to warn off predators. The larvae feed only on milk parsley.

ACTUAL SIZE

Swallowtails were once common in many British marshlands, but are now found only in the marshes around the Norfolk Broads.

FACT FILE

Scientific name *Papilio machaon*

Habitat Marshland

Breeding Eggs are laid in several broods from April to September and they may hatch the same year, or the next

Wingspan Up to 8 cm

Yellow wings with black veins

Long, black tails

Hind wings have a band of blue and a red spot

WALL BROWN

Often found resting on walls in direct sunlight, wall browns soak up warmth from the sun's rays. Males are more active than females but look similar. These butterflies are not fussy feeders and take nectar from a range of flowers. They were once widespread, except in Scotland, but their numbers have dropped dramatically.

Insects cannot warm their own bodies, so they rely on sunshine. When a wall brown is warm, it can fly, feed and mate more easily.

FACT FILE

Scientific name
Lasiommata megera
Habitat Coastal areas, wastelands and hedgerows
Breeding Round eggs are often laid on grass, and the larvae are green
Wingspan 4.5 to 5.5 cm

Long body with slender abdomen

Bold, orange and brown-black patterns

White-grey fringe

WHITE ADMIRAL

These butterflies have few habitats to chose from because their larvae only feed on honeysuckle plants. White admirals live in woodlands of southern England, and the species is quite rare. Females are slightly bigger than males, but look similar. They lay just one egg at a time on honeysuckle in sheltered places. Adults are strong fliers and glide between trees.

ACTUAL SIZE

The larvae make silk and use it to 'glue' leaves to twigs creating a nest to spend the winter in.

FACT FILE

Scientific name
Limenitis camilla

Habitat Woodlands

Breeding Light, brown larvae emerge from small, hairy eggs

Wingspan 5.5 to 6.5 cm

Antennae tips are orange

Broad, black wings

There may be small patches of red or blue on the wings

White banding across wings

ANGLE SHADES

These stunning moths can be difficult to spot. When angle shades are at rest, their folded wings resemble dead or decaying leaves. Dark bands of colour also help angle shades to remain camouflaged and out of sight. They are active in both the day and the night. Young larvae are often the colour of their food plants, which helps them to avoid predators.

ACTUAL SIZE

Adults can be seen throughout the year, although they are more common in summer. Larvae rest through the winter.

FACT FILE

Scientific name
Phlogophora meticulosa
Habitat Parks, fields, coastal areas and gardens
Breeding Two broods of eggs may be laid in one year and the larvae are brown or green
Wingspan 4–6 cm

Slender antennae

Furry body

Wings can appear wrinkled, like a dead leaf

Young adults have bands of green, pink or brown on their wings

BRIMSTONE

Small, pretty brimstone moths are a distinctive yellow colour. Their wings are marked with small, brown patches, especially along the front edges of the forewings. Brimstones are most active at night, and they fly towards windows and other sources of light. They are most common from spring to autumn. The larvae feast on a range of bushes and other plants.

ACTUAL SIZE

The larvae of brimstones can be green or brown. The brown larvae look like twigs and are very difficult to spot when they are still.

FACT FILE

Scientific name
Opisthograptis luteolata
Habitat Gardens, woodlands, fields and parks
Breeding Up to two broods a year in southern Britain, but just one in northern places
Wingspan 3–4 cm

Wings are leaf-shaped

Yellow, rounded body

Antennae dip downwards

Orange-brown patches on forewings

Wing colour may be yellow or deep cream

CINNABAR

With their black and red wings, cinnabars are very distinctive. They rest in low-lying plants during the day and become active at dusk. Cinnabars lay their eggs on ragwort plants in June, and hairy, striped larvae hatch from July onwards. Gold and black stripes on the larvae warn other animals that they taste bad. The larvae form pupae in September and spend winter resting.

ACTUAL SIZE

Cinnabar is a bright-red mineral that is sometimes used as a pigment. This moth is named after the mineral because of its red markings.

FACT FILE

Scientific name *Tyria jacobaeae*

Habitat Heaths, wastelands, grassy areas and woodlands

Breeding Adults produce one brood from May to July and the larvae feed mostly on ragwort

Wingspan 3.5–4 cm

Forewings are grey-black with red markings

Black body and legs

Hind wings are red with black borders

CODLING

The larvae of codling moths are pests that eat the fruit of some trees, particularly apple and pear. Adult females lay a single egg on a leaf of the tree. When the larva emerges, it bores into apples or pears, making long tunnels as it eats its way through the fruit flesh. The larva pupates under bark or in leaf litter, emerging as an adult between November and February, depending on the conditions.

ACTUAL SIZE

The large eye-shaped markings on the tips of the forewings distract and confuse predators, such as birds.

FACT FILE

Scientific name
Cydia pomonella

Habitat Where apple trees grow

Breeding Larvae are also known as apple maggots, and they have white bodies and brown heads

Wingspan 1–2 cm

Grey head and body

Grey-and-brown mottled wings

Copper-coloured bands

Large eyes made up of many small lenses

COMMON EMERALD

The green colour of common emerald moths make them easy to identify, although the colour fades through the summer. These moths are usually spotted in June and July in southern UK, especially around sunset when they emerge from their hiding places. They are rare in northern regions. The larvae feed on a range of shrubs, especially redcurrant, rowan, hawthorn and blackthorn.

ACTUAL SIZE

The larvae are able to survive the winter. They can be found as larvae or pupae from August to May, on a range of trees and shrubs.

FACT FILE

Scientific name
Hemithea aestivaria

Habitat Woodlands, gardens and parks

Breeding The larvae are green or brown, and stick-like

Wingspan 3 cm

Long, delicate antennae

White lines may be visible on the wings

Hind wings have distinctive angles

DEATH'S HEAD HAWK-MOTH

This striking moth gets its name from the unusual pattern on the back of its thorax. This is the part of the body between the head and the fleshy abdomen. Also known as a 'death's head', the pattern resembles a skull. These moths migrate to Britain for the summer. The larvae feed on potato plants, so the adults are most likely to be found in farms.

SCALE

These moths have the strange habit of crawling into beehives in search of honey. They can produce a loud, squeaking noise if they are handled or startled.

FACT FILE

Scientific name
Acherontia atropos
Habitat Farmland
Breeding The pale-green larvae have purple and white stripes, and can grow up to 15 cm in length
Wingspan Up to 14 cm

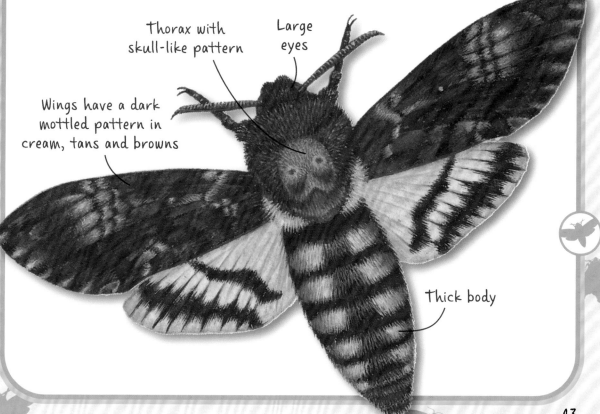

Thorax with skull-like pattern

Large eyes

Wings have a dark mottled pattern in cream, tans and browns

Thick body

ELEPHANT HAWK-MOTH

These beautiful, colourful moths can easily be mistaken for pink butterflies. However, their fat bodies and triangular shape means they are classed as moths. They are active at night, feeding on nectar from fuchsia, rhododendron and honeysuckle plants. The larvae have large eye-spots on their head-end, but are harmless despite their fearsome appearance.

ACTUAL SIZE

This moth is said to get its name from the way the larvae look like an elephant's trunk. They are wide at one end and taper to the other.

FACT FILE

Scientific name
Deilephila elpenor
Habitat Gardens and woodlands
Breeding The large larvae hide in the ground and pupate over the winter, emerging in spring
Wingspan 7 cm

Wings create a characteristic triangle shape

Bright pink, olive green and brown forewings

Brightly coloured, plump body

Dark patches on hind wings are sometimes visible

FEATHERED THORN

Unlike most other British moths and butterflies, feathered thorn adults do not emerge in summer. They have a short season, from September to December, when they must mate and lay their eggs, and they have just one brood. These moths are most often found in woodlands with broad-leaved trees, such as sycamore and oak. They are named after the males' feathery antennae.

ACTUAL SIZE

The males' feathery antennae are used to locate females. They are able to detect the chemicals produced by females, even some distance away.

FACT FILE

Scientific name
Colotois pennaria
Habitat Woodlands, gardens and parks
Breeding Eggs are laid on trees and survive the winter, hatching in spring
Wingspan 3.5–4.5 cm

Thorax is very hairy, but abdomen is mostly hidden from view

Males have large, feathery antennae

Small, white spots near wing tips

Orange-brown wings with some dark banding

GARDEN CARPET

These moths favour gardens and parks where they can find crucifer plants for their larvae to feed on. The larvae usually only feed at night, so it can be hard to find them. Garden carpet moths may survive the winter, either as larvae or pupae. The larvae build silken cocoons in soil. Adults emerge in April and are active through the summer.

ACTUAL SIZE

The larvae can be a range of colours, from white to pinkish, green or brown. The head is yellowish-brown.

FACT FILE

Scientific name
Xanthorhoe fluctuata

Habitat Gardens, parks and woodlands

Breeding Can produce several broods from April to October

Wingspan 2–3 cm

The base colour is creamy-white

Mottled patterns and colours on wings

Rests with its wings flat

GARDEN TIGER

With their bold colours, garden tiger moths are easy to spot. The red-coloured hind wings warn other animals to leave them alone, as they taste bad. Garden tigers feed on nectar from flowers. The larvae are brown and black, and are so hairy that they have been named 'woolly bears'. The hairs cause irritation, so they protect the larvae from hungry birds.

ACTUAL SIZE

Garden tiger moths vary in appearance. It is rare to find two moths with the same markings.

FACT FILE

Scientific name *Arctia caja*

Habitat Gardens, farms and open areas

Breeding
Black and orange larvae

Wingspan 6 cm

Long, feathery antennae

Fluffy thorax

Large forewings are patterned in black-brown and cream

Fat abdomen

Hind wings are red-orange with black-and-blue markings

LIME HAWK

These moths can be identified by their wing shape, as well as their markings. Lime hawk moths are common in towns and cities, especially from May onwards. The adults do not feed, but the larvae feed on leaves, particularly those of lime trees. Most larvae are green and have yellow stripes. The colours deepen as the larvae age and prepare to pupate.

SCALE

These moths are named after the lime trees that the larvae feed on, which grow in towns and cities, especially in southern Britain.

FACT FILE

Scientific name *Mimas tiliae*

Habitat Woodlands and gardens

Breeding Eggs are laid on trees such as lime, elm, birch and elder

Wingspan 6–8 cm

The colours can vary, but the base colour is usually pinkish

Olive-green or brown blotches

Wings have a scalloped edge

MAGPIE

Boldly patterned magpie moths have black-and-white wings with yellow bands. This colouring warns predators, such as birds and spiders, that they taste bad. Adults emerge from their pupae in June and drink nectar from flowers. They can be seen until August and, unlike many other moths, they are active during the day.

Magpie moth larvae also have bold colouring to keep predators away. Even spiders hate the taste of these insects, and their venom seems to have no effect on the moths.

FACT FILE

Scientific name
Abraxas grossulariata

Habitat Meadows and woods

Breeding One brood a year and larvae survive the winter

Wingspan 4–5 cm

Long antennae

Forewings are white with black bands and spots

Yellow band crosses the forewings

POPLAR HAWK

Regularly visiting gardens, large poplar hawk moths are common in Britain. When these moths are at rest, the hind wings are positioned in front of the forewings, giving it an unusual appearance. The larvae are green and have a small tail horn. Older caterpillars have diagonal yellow stripes on their green bodies. They feed on poplar, aspen and willow trees.

SCALE

Adults have a proboscis for feeding, but it is never used. Like many other adult moths, poplar hawks do not feed once they have emerged from the pupae.

FACT FILE

Scientific name *Laothoe populi*

Habitat Woodlands and gardens

Breeding Usually just one brood a year, but occasionally a second brood emerges in late summer

Wingspan Up to 9 cm

A reddish patch on the hind wing is flashed at predators

Colours may be yellow-brown, reddish, brown or even grey

Hind wing

When at rest, the abdomen curls upwards slightly

Forewing

PRIVET HAWK-MOTH

Hawk-moths are usually large and excellent fliers, and these moths are no exception. They are common in southern regions of Britain, visiting gardens in search of privet bushes – the favourite food of their larvae. Privet hawk-moths can be seen resting in the sun during June and July. The larvae are very large and fleshy. Their skin is bright green with delicate white and lilac diagonal stripes.

SCALE

Male privet hawk–moths make a hissing noise when disturbed. This may scare predators away.

FACT FILE

Scientific name *Sphinx ligustri*

Habitat Gardens and woodlands

Breeding Just one brood of eggs is laid every year, usually in June or July

Wingspan 9–12 cm

Slender antennae

Striped hind wings are sometimes hidden from view

Large body has pink and black bars

SCALLOPED OAK

Living in a wide range of habitats, scalloped oak moths are widespread throughout Britain. Adults emerge from their pupae in summer and fly during July and August. They lay a single brood of eggs, normally on broad-leaved plants such as hawthorn, which becomes the food for the larvae. It is difficult to spot the larvae because they are twig-like and well camouflaged in a leafy bush or tree.

ACTUAL SIZE

Some pale-coloured moths, including scalloped oaks, occasionally appear in much darker forms. They are described as 'melanic'.

FACT FILE

Scientific name
Crocallis elinguaria
Habitat Gardens, parks, fields and woodlands
Breeding Eggs survive over the winter and twig-like larvae hatch in spring
Wingspan 4–5 cm

Colour can vary from lemon-yellow to brown

Black spot on forewings

Hind wings are plain and paler in colour

SCARLET TIGER

These moths live in damp habitats in central and southern regions of England and Wales. The favourite food of their larvae is the comfrey plant, although they also eat brambles and nettles. Scarlet tiger moths are active in the day, feeding on nectar, which they suck from flowers. Their forewings are shiny, which is an unusual feature in moths, although common in butterflies.

ACTUAL SIZE

Scarlet tiger larvae are easy to spot. They have black bodies with a white or yellow stripe along their backs, as well as rows of spots and stripes.

FACT FILE

Scientific name
Callimorpha dominula

Habitat Damp places especially marshes, fens and riverbanks

Breeding One brood is laid every year, and the larvae are hairy

Wingspan 4–6 cm

Greenish-black base colour on forewings

Rare colours, such as yellow, may be seen

A green metallic sheen on the forewings

Scarlet hind wings

SIX-SPOT BURNET

The plump, yellow larvae of six-spot burnet moths feed on bird's foot trefoil. This wild flower contains a deadly chemical, called cyanide, which collects in the larva's body. When the larva becomes an adult, it is still poisonous to eat, and the bright-red spots on its wings warn predators to stay away. These moths are active during the day and feed on nectar. They fly from June to August and their larvae can survive the winter.

ACTUAL SIZE

The six-spot burnet can be found in grasslands throughout England, but in other places it is mostly found in coastal regions.

FACT FILE

Scientific name
Zygaena filipendulae
Habitat Meadows, grasslands and coastal areas
Breeding One brood every year and the larvae form yellow pupae on grass stems
Wingspan 3–4 cm

Long antennae

Forewings are black with a bluish sheen

Six scarlet spots on each forewing

Red hind wings with a black fringe

SWALLOW-TAILED

Although swallow-tailed moths are widespread throughout Britain, except the most northern parts, they are rarely seen. The adults fly for just a few weeks in July and are active at night. The slender larvae stay camouflaged among ivy – one of their food plants. One brood of eggs is produced each year, and the larvae feed from August to the following June.

With its delicate wings, pale-yellow colour and dainty, orange banding, this moth can easily be mistaken for a butterfly.

FACT FILE

Scientific name
Ourapteryx sambucaria

Habitat Woodland, gardens, fields, hedgerows and parks

Breeding Small, lilac eggs hatch to produce twig-like larvae

Wingspan 4–6 cm

Yellow body

Wings are pale lemon-yellow with thin banding

The hind wings have prominent points, or 'tails'

GLOSSARY

Abdomen The rear part of an insect's body, behind the head and thorax.

Antennae (singular: antenna) A pair of structures on an insect's head, sensitive to smell, sound and touch.

Aphid A tiny bug that sucks liquid from inside a plant.

Brood All the young insects that hatch at the same time.

Camouflage The way that an animal's colour, markings or shape enables it to blend in with its surroundings.

Chrysalises (singular: chrysalis) The hard cases that protect the pupae of butterflies or moths.

Cocoon A silken case spun by a larva to protect itself while it pupates.

Compound eyes Eyes that are made up of many small lenses.

Eye-spot Coloured and patterned scales that look like an eye.

Gland A special part of the body that makes chemical substances, such as scents.

Habitat The natural home of a plant or an animal.

Heath An area of open land with low-growing plants, such as heather, grass and gorse.

Hibernation A period of time spent resting over the winter.

Larvae (singular: larva) The first stage of an insect's life-cycle after hatching from its egg.

Life expectancy The length of time an animal is expected to live under normal circumstances.

Moor An open area of high land where grasses, heather and similar plants grow wild.

Nectar A sugary substance produced by flowering plants to attract insects.

Nutrient A food substance that allows a living thing to grow and survive.

Pigment A chemical that gives colour to an animal or plant.

Predator An animal that hunts other animals to eat.

Proboscis A long, slender mouthpart of butterflies and moths. It works by absorbing liquid, not sucking it.

Pupa (plural: pupae) The resting stage of an insect's life-cycle, when it changes from a larva to an adult.

Shrub A woody plant that is smaller than a tree.

Species A group of similar living things that can breed together.

Territory The space that an animal defends from other animals.

Thorax The body part of an insect that lies between its head and abdomen. Wings (if there are any) and legs are attached to the thorax.